Hong Kong
Life and Times

Page 4 : A sign of the times, the Bank of China dominates the Central business district of Hong Kong.
Pages 6-7: The Chinese dragon, symbol of power and authority, soars through the skies of Hong Kong.

PHOTO CREDITS

Luca Invernizzi Tettoni, Photobank: 10, 11, 16, 18, 22 (right), 23, 24-25, 26, 27 (left), 28, 29 (top & bottom, left), 33 (top right), 37 (top left and right), 41 (top), 44, 46, 48, 49 (top & bottom left), 52 (top left),54 (top), 56, 57 (top left), 58 (top), 59, 60, 61, 62 (top left & right, bottom right), 63 (right), 67 (right), 70 (bottom right), 71, 72, 73, 75 (top), 76-77, 78 (right), 80 (left & right), 84 (right), 85 (bottom right), 93, 94 (top left & right), 95, 99 (top left), 102, 104 (bottom right), 105, 111 (top right); Hong Kong Tourist Association: 29 (top right), 36, 37 (bottom), 39, 50, 51, 52 (top right, bottom left & right), 53, 54 (bottom right), 55, 57 (bottom left & right), 58 (bottom), 87, 88, 89, 90, 91, 96 (right), 97 (top), 99 (top right, bottom left & right), 104 (top); Chris Davis: 17 (bottom left & right), 19, 21 (bottom right), 32, 33 (left & bottom right), 38 (top left & right), 40, 41 (bottom), 43 (left), 49 (bottom right), 67 (left), 78 (top left), 79 (top), 82 (top left & bottom), 100 (top & bottom left), 104 (bottom left), 107 (top right & bottom); Renata Holzbachova/Philippe Bennet: 21 (top left), 64 (centre top left, bottom right), 65, 70 (top & bottom left), 74 (top left & centre, bottom left), 75 (bottom), 85 (top left & right), 92, 97 (bottom), 100 (bottom right), 101, 111(top left, bottom left & right), 112; The Image Bank: 6-7, 17 (top), 22 (top left), 35, 45, 47 (top), 57 (top right), 62 (bottom left), 66, 68 (top left & right), 69 (left), 74 (far top right), 78 (bottom left), 79 (bottom left & right), 82 (right) 83, 94 (bottom), 98, 103 (bottom left & right), 107 (left); International Photobank: 20, 21 (bottom left), 22 (bottom left), 30, 31, 86, 96 (left); HBL Network Photo Agency: 21 (top right), 27 (right), 42, 43 (right), 47 (bottom), 63 (left), 64 (top), 68 (bottom left), 69 (right), 74 (bottom right), 81 (right), 84 (left), 85 (bottom left), 110; R.G.B. Photo Library: 34, 38 (bottom left), 64 (bottom left), 103 (top), 106, 108-109, Bes Stock: 4; The Hulton-Deutsch Collection: 8, 12, 13, 14, 15; Courtesy of The Hong Kong and Shanghai Banking Corporation Limited; Hong Kong Museum of History: 124 (top), 127 (bottom); Richard Garrett: 120, 121 (bottom); Anne Selby: 113, 114, 115, 116, 117, 118, 119, 121 (top), 122, 123, 124, (bottom), 125, 126, 127 (top), 128.

HONG KONG: LIFE AND TIMES

Published by Times Editions
an imprint of Times Editions Pte Ltd
Times Centre, 1 New Industrial Road
Singapore 536196

Project Editor: K E Tan
Designer: Felicia Wong
Production Manager: Anthoney Chua
Colour separation by Colour Scan Pte Ltd, Singapore
Printed by Times Offset (M) Sdn. Bhd.

ISBN: 981 204 734 4

HONG KONG
LIFE AND TIMES

Text by Valery M. Garrett

TIMES EDITIONS

Sanwa Bank

CONTENTS

INTRODUCTION

On June 30th 1997, as the calendar turns, another chapter in the history of a once glorious British empire will close. For 156 years, 5 months and 10 days, life in this tiny outpost on the south China coast has been governed, not by imperial rulers in Beijing, but by mandarins of a different colour and creed in faraway London. At the stroke of twelve on that warm summer night, the Union Jack will be slowly lowered, and the book on Hong Kong returned to the shelf marked China.

In real terms this period of colonial rule will seem like the blink of an eye for there were settlers here 6,000 years ago. But this tiny island, just inside the Tropic of Cancer, seldom appeared on the map before the British claimed her for their own in 1841. Slowly, with a blend of dogged British bureaucracy and a hefty dose of hard work from freedom seekers from China, it became a mecca for entrepreneurs, businessmen and captains of industry.

It seemed an unpromising choice in the beginning. Opium, that infamous commodity used

Reclamation is a constant fact of life in Hong Kong. Here in 1890 the Praya (facing page), in the Central district of the island, is being extended. When the work was completed in 1904, the original Praya was renamed Des Voeux Road in memory of Sir William Des Voeux, Governor of Hong Kong from 1887 to 1891.

Above: Dr William Jardine, founder of one of the big hongs or trading houses. In 1832 Jardine, a ship's surgeon and his partner, James Matheson, founded the firm which still bears their name today, Jardine, Matheson & Co.

Left: An early view in oils of Hong Kong island by a Chinese artist in the 1880s as seen from the mainland.

Artists were dispatched from London to record aspects of the new British colony. The Illustrated London News *and the* Graphic *were two newspapers which published impressions of life in Hong Kong. Barbers, fortune-tellers, letter writers and hawkers all carried out their trades on the streets of the Chinese quarter of town. Opium smoking was an accepted distraction and continued into the 20th century.*

Sedan chairs were the only form of transport able to scale the hills of Victoria Peak until the funicular railway was built in 1888. Chairs for the general public had two bearers but senior members of the government and wealthy merchants had their own four, six or eight bearers dressed in company livery. The last sedan chair was found abandoned on the street in the 1960s.

Facing page: The signature page of the Treaty of Nanking signed on August 29, 1842 aboard the British flagship HMS Cornwallis *anchored in the Yangzi river near the city of Nanking. This Treaty ceded Hong Kong island in perpetuity to 'Her Britannic Majesty, Queen Victoria, Her heirs and Her successors'.*

by western nations to purchase tea, porcelain and silk from China, had been banned by the Chinese government in 1839. Crippled with defeat in the ensuing war, China yielded to Britain's demands for a base of her own from which to trade, instead of being confined to Portuguese-governed Macau. The island of Hong Kong, chosen by Captain Charles Elliot, was duly taken on 26th January 1841. However, far from being praised, Elliot was banished in disgrace as the island was scornfully described by Foreign Secretary, Lord Palmerston, as "a barren rock with nary a house upon it". Queen Victoria was not amused.

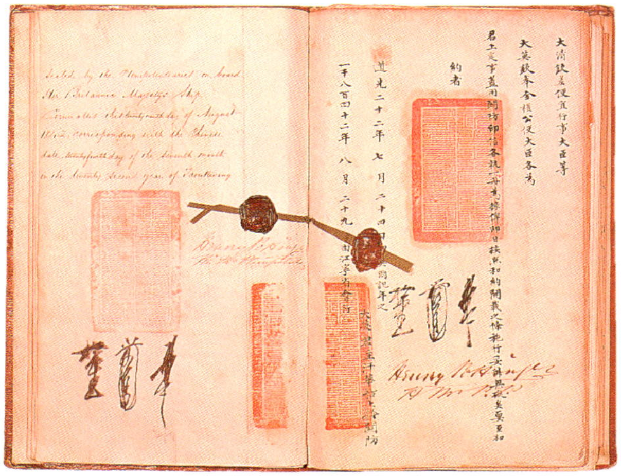

However, settlement soon began, the city of Victoria developed and the importance of the natural deepwater harbour was quickly realised. In 1860, a little over 6 sq km of the Kowloon peninsula on the opposite side of the water became British following another "unequal" pact with the Manchu rulers of China, themselves intruders since 1644. Then in 1898, as more land was needed, the decision was made to lease 565 sq km of land from Boundary Street in Kowloon up to the Shenzhen River, together with another 234 islands, for a period of 99 years.

With the end of the lease approaching the Sino-British agreement was signed in 1984, the result being that all of Hong Kong territory will be handed back to China in 1997. Hong Kong will then become a Special Administrative Region (SAR) of China, autonomous under a 50-year "one-government, two-systems" guarantee, taking it through to 2047.

Today the population stands at 6.3 million, a far cry from less than 6,000 in a handful of villages on Hong Kong island back in 1841. Ninety-three per cent of the population are Chinese, most from the neighbouring southern provinces of Guangdong and Fujian, but increasingly from northern China too as 1997 approaches. The remaining 7 per cent expatriate population are from nearby South-east Asian countries, as well as North America, Britain, Europe and the Antipodes.

At first glance it seems Hong Kong has embraced western culture as though she had invented it. English is the official language, along with Cantonese. The traffic flows on the left. Cricket is still played, designer fashions from France and Italy fill the boutiques and clothe the *tai tais*. Afternoon tea is served to the accompaniment of a tinkling piano in all the best hotels.

Queen's Road, named after the ruling Queen Victoria, in 1880 (left). Already substantial colonial buildings line the main thoroughfare. Today it is one of the busiest streets in Hong Kong.
Centre, left: Queen Victoria's memorial in Royal Square, now called Statue Square, was erected to mark her jubilee in 1887.
Below, bottom left and right and facing page: Commerce makes the wheels go round in Hong Kong. Here, at the fishing ports in the 1960s, goods arrive daily from China while fish is sold fresh from the sea. Cheongsam clad girls contemplate a purchase in a goldsmith's shop, street markets are thronged with customers and a young entrepreneur dreams of the day he will be a millionaire.

廣源酒店
實用

THE "STAR" FERRY Co. Ltd.
KOWLOON FERRY

KOWLOON POST OFFICE

A rickshaw puller in the 1950s runs down Chater Road while others rest as they wait for passengers (facing page, top left and bottom left). The rickshaw was invented in the 1870s by an American missionary in Tokyo whose wife was appalled by the inhuman labour of the sedan chair coolies. The rickshaw soon caught on and was introduced into Hong Kong from 1874. In 1924 there were 3,411 registered though the number dropped off in the 1930s. Nineteen seventy five was the last year licences were issued and only twenty applied.

Facing page, top right and bottom right: The Star Ferry Company, pictured in 1949, carried passengers across the harbour to Kowloon station where they could board a train to the New Territories, Guangzhou, or right across Asia to Paris and London arriving a mere 18 days later.

Outside the railway terminal long lines of buses stand idle. Anti-British demonstrations by supporters of the Communist regime in Beijing in the summer of 1967 caused the Star Ferry to go on strike, together with buses and taxis and other utilities.

This page: The Kowloon Canton Railway (KCR) British section opened in October 1910 and the Chinese section was completed one year later. Here, soon after its opening, passengers wait under the British flag at the railway bridge at Lo Wu, the border between the New Territories and China.

By the 1960s the bamboo curtain was down. A Chinese guard on the bridge bars the way and entry into China was severely restricted.

But don't be fooled. Scratch the surface and Hong Kong is Chinese through and through. Traditional festivals continue to flourish. Chinese opera can draw bigger crowds than Oscar winning movies. The almanac is checked for favourable days on which to marry, move house, or even, by some, on when to get a haircut. In the middle of the city, as well as in the countryside of the New Territories, ancient temples are in constant use as gods and ancestors are consulted on how to gain wealth and good fortune.

In the last twenty-five years Hong Kong has moved rapidly from being a quiet colonial backwater into the fast international lane. Now a major power in the world's financial markets, she is a cosmopolitan city with first-class hotels, glittering shopping malls and some of the most expensive real estate. With one foot rooted in ancient Chinese beliefs and another firmly set in the future, Hong Kong is truly a sparkling jewel in the shining South China Sea.

Government House (top) was first built in 1853 and acquired a unique blend of Japanese and European styles when it was remodelled by the Japanese Governor during the occupation of Hong Kong in the Second World War. The 28th and final Governor of Hong Kong to be appointed by Britain, the Right Honourable Chris Patten (bottom right) ponders his next move, while British-born but longtime Hong Kong resident, Elsie Tu (bottom left), speaks out on behalf of the grass roots population.

Facing page: Hong Kong people take a keener interest in local politics faced with the imminent return of the territory to a Communist-led country from which many of their families fled. Pro-democracy rallies such as this one are more common these days and democracy has become a hotly debated issue though many remain firmly against the idea.

WATERFRONT AND HARBOUR

In Cantonese, Hong Kong means fragrant harbour and the harbour is still where the action takes place today. The waterfront continually changes as reclamation narrows the gap between the island and Kowloon. Fishing junks in full sail are a rare sight nowadays but the green and white hulls of the Star Ferry continue to carry passengers across the harbour as they have for almost 100 years. Dodging the ocean liners and ferries to outlying islands are bouncing hoverferries and jetfoils zipping back and forth to Macau, while loaded lighters make their way slowly from ship to shore.

Beyond the sweep of the Hong Kong Cultural Centre in Kowloon, the skyscrapers on Hong Kong island glitter in the noonday sun against the hills of Victoria Peak (facing page). Harbour front land is among the world's most expensive real estate. Below: The firing of the Noon Day Gun takes place every day in Causeway Bay. The tradition began last century when Jardines welcomed its taipans *with a double gun salute. A naval officer took exception as gun salutes were only allowed for high ranking officers. As a penalty Jardines were ordered to fire a gun at noon every day henceforth as a time signal for Hong Kong people.*

The twin towers of the Shun Tak Centre (above) where jetfoils leave every 15 minutes for Macau, 64 km and an hour away on the other side of the Pearl River estuary. Macau has been Portuguese territory since 1557 and will be returned to China in 1999.
Facing page: The Star Ferry has made the eight minute crossing of the harbour from Hong Kong to Kowloon since 1898. All twelve vessels with their distinctive two decker green and white hulls are named after stars, such as Twinkling, Celestial or Meridian, and transport over 40 million passengers per year. They have featured in nearly all the movies ever made on Hong Kong and a ride must be the best value for money anywhere in the world. Outside the ferry terminal, rickshaw pullers snooze as they wait for passengers.

PHILIPS
SAMSUNG
CELESTIAL STAR
HONG KONG

Motorised fishing junks and sampans crowd the typhoon anchorage at Causeway Bay (this page). The boats are home to many thousands of fishing people who live their whole life at sea. Facing page: A Tanka fisherwoman rows her sampan. Thought to be a race of seagoing gypsies, the Tankas were forbidden to live ashore, enter the imperial civil service examinations or to marry land dwellers during the Qing dynasty. Nowadays they have the same rights as the land population.

Following pages: The skyline of Hong Kong island in the early evening looking west towards Causeway Bay anchorage, Central district and Victoria Peak.

SOGO

Canon

The business districts in Central and Wanchai glitter like gold mines (facing page and left). The Hong Kong Convention and Exhibition Centre, seen on the left on the opposite page, is currently being extended. This is where the ceremony of handing over Hong Kong to China will take place in July 1997.
Above: The newly constructed Tsing Ma bridge, crossing from Tsing Yi island to Ma Wan, leads the way to the new airport at Chek Lap Kok on the northern shore of Lantau island and due to open in 1998.

Aberdeen harbour is one of the oldest fishing ports in Hong Kong. In the past, boat people would be born, married and die on their boat, although these days children attend school on land and many have been settled ashore in high-rise apartments.

Sampans ferry fishing people to the shore as they stock up on daily necessities before setting out to sea again. Nowadays they must sail further and further up and down the coast in search of a good catch, away for several days at a time. Aberdeen is a popular place for visitors too as they take the short trip from the floating restaurant round the bustling harbour.

Back home from the sea, the day's catch dries in the sun, ready for the larder. There's a faraway look in the fisherman's eyes as he gazes out to sea. In the fishmarket, buyers haggle over prices. An old Tanka fisherwoman wears her distinctive deep brimmed hat to shade her eyes as she sets off to market.

Cargo operations began here in Kwai Chung more than twenty-five years ago, and now the container terminal is the busiest in the world, overtaking New York and Rotterdam. The site covers more than 160 hectares with eight Terminals, and others are in the pipeline. Apart from the regular type of cargo, more unusual consignments have included zoo animals, live pigs, and less welcome, a container holding illegal immigrants from China. This was one shipment which failed to reach its destination as all were captured and returned across the border.

MTL
OCL
OCL

HUD
HUD

RURAL RHYTHMS

The first permanent settlers in the flat fertile plains of the New Territories were the Five Great Clans who arrived from central China between the 10th and the 15th centuries. Establishing themselves in walled villages as protection against pirates and other marauders, these Cantonese landowners became very wealthy. Later the Hakkas, whose name means guest people, arrived in the 18th and 19th centuries, escaping from disturbances in northern China. Although the increase in population since the war has meant that many of the old market towns have grown dramatically in size, there are still places where the seasonal rhythms carry on undisturbed as they have for centuries.

An old Hakka villager chews thoughtfully on her pipe (facing page). The straw hat with the deep black fringe is still worn by the Hakka women and does a good job in shielding the face from flies or the sun.
Below: Bicycles are a convenient means of transporting produce to market.

In the past there were many duck farms in the shallow bays along the border with China, but nowadays very few remain. Rice, fit for an emperor's table, is no longer grown in the New Territories but some fish farms continue and vegetables are still tended for the market.

The pungent aroma of a paste made from dried shrimps accosts the visitor in some villages along the coast of the New Territories.

The Tangs were the earliest of the Five Great Clans to arrive in the New Territories when their founding ancestor settled here back in the Song dynasty. Their walled village, Kat Ling Wai at Kam Tin, was first built 600 years ago and about 400 members of the family still live within its walls. There were once over forty walled villages in the New Territories, built as defence against pirates and rival villages, but now only a handful remain.

Kat Ling Wai is a regular stop for tourists and the elderly women sell souvenirs to add to their income. A visitor (bottom left) dresses up in traditional straw hat and jacket.

More than forty per cent of Hong Kong territory is given over to country parks such as Sai Kung (facing page). Here, it is possible to walk for miles without seeing another soul. Ferries are the main means of transport to these remote outlying areas.
Above and left: The fishing village of Tai O at the tip of Lantau island. Tanka and the other group of fisherpeople, the Hoklo, who originated from Fujian province, live in homes built on stilts, giving them the feeling they are still living on water.

Small boats cross the many creeks and waterways of Tai O.

Back in the eastern New Territories the Taiwan flag of the Republic of China flutters at Rennies Mill, inhabited since 1950 by pro-Guomintang refugees. With the handover to China growing closer, the land has now been reclaimed by the government and the inhabitants resettled.

C R E E D S   A N D   C U S T O M S

To those brought up believing in one faith or deity, Chinese religion can be a confusing and complex affair. Daoism is the oldest belief dating from the 5th century B.C. It teaches the way to eternal life through the understanding of natural processes, the balance of Yin and Yang, and the harmony of man and nature. Daoists strive for patience, simplicity and contentment. Most people also acquire some measure of Buddhist faith, but at the same time believe in animism and other religious elements. In fact, many devotees pray to every deity in the conviction that the more deities worshipped, the more favours granted. But ancestor worship is the most important and deep-seated belief with offerings made in return for spiritual favours.

A man pays homage to the deities in the Man Mo temple in Hollywood Road (facing page). Built in 1847, the name literally means "civil and martial" and is dedicated to two Daoist gods, Man Cheung, the god of literature, and Kwan Kung, the god of martial arts. It is the city temple for Hong Kong island and a centre for local people, as can seen by the numerous incense coils lit to ask for favours from the gods. Left: Fortune sticks are thrown to determine whether the wish will come true. The number on the stick corresponds with a paper containing a parable, the predictions being divined by the temple keeper.

On the many festival days throughout the year, all the temples round the territory are packed with worshippers burning incense sticks and making offerings to the gods. Sometimes called joss sticks, joss being a corruption of the Portuguese word deos *or idol, the sticks are burned in groups of three: one for heaven, one for earth and one for all mankind.*

Situated on Lantau island, a one-hour ferry ride from Hong Kong, is the Po Lin monastery set amid spectacular scenery on top of Ngong Ping mountain (above left). This is the site of the world's tallest outdoor bronze Buddha. Completed in 1990 the 34-metre high statue, weighing 250 tonnes, is Hong Kong's most prominent religious symbol, and, on a clear day, visible for miles around.

Above right: A monk walks through the tranquil grounds of the monastery which was established in 1927 and is a major centre of Buddhism in Hong Kong.

The Qing Ming festival held in the spring is one of two annual holidays in the year when descendants honour the dead. This Confucian celebration dates back to the Han dynasty (206 B.C.-A.D. 221). All Chinese cemeteries are very busy on this day as graves are swept, washed, and newly painted. The family will present offerings of roast pig, poultry, oranges and wine which are afterwards consumed at the graveside. Incense sticks and gold and silver "money" is burned to give the ancestors enough to spend in the afterworld. Urns holding the bones of ancestors are temporary resting places until a permanent burial site is found, but must still be worshipped.

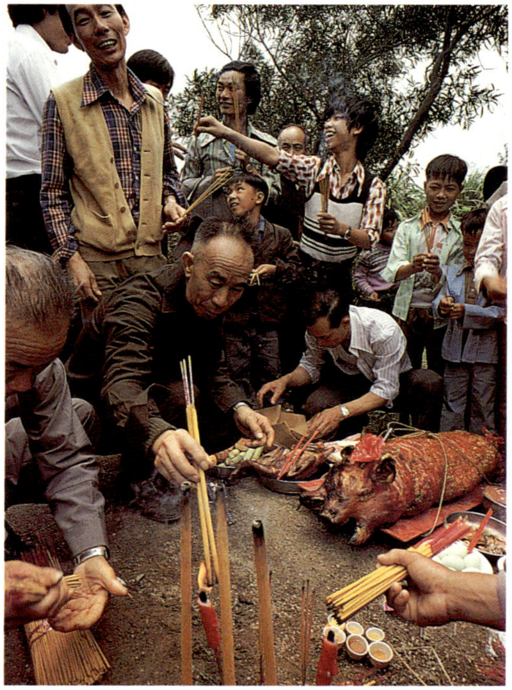

醮
酧謝神恩
錦田吉慶圍全体同人
敬賀
酧謝神恩
敬賀

The Da Jiu ceremony (left and facing page) is held usually at ten year intervals in many large villages in the New Territories. Literally "purification rituals for peace", the festival is a thanks for past blessings, a prayer for future prosperity and peace, and a community wide exorcism of ghosts and evil. Huge ceremonial archways called paai-lau *are presented by different organisations to congratulate the village. Made of brightly coloured paper flowers stuck on a bamboo framework in striking patterns and designs, they feature dragons and other lucky symbols for the auspicious ceremony.*

Hundreds of clan members return to the home village from all points of the globe. Every god which inhabits the village and surrounding countryside must be brought to the ceremony and given a seat of honour. Daoist priests in red robes officiate, reading out loud the names of everyone who participates at the festival. The long list will be burned and sent to heaven on the back of a paper horse. The whole ceremony lasts for almost a week and will cost several million Hong Kong dollars.

一年之計在於春
舉國更生憑自力

The three-day celebrations at Chinese New Year fall, according to the lunar calendar, sometime between mid-January and mid-February. Lucky couplets are renewed on New Year's Eve and door gods, posters of fierce warriors whose task it is to prevent evil from entering the home, are pasted up. Over the three days firecrackers are set off, laisee *packets are given to the unmarried, and everyone wishes each other* gung hei faat choi *"best wishes and get rich!". The 200-foot long dancing dragon, made in many separate sections, is manoeuvred by young men who cause it to sway and undulate. As the dragon passes through the villages, ducking in and out of doorways, it dispels evil and brings good fortune.*

Fragrant peach trees, symbols of longevity and good fortune, decorate the homes and offices. Farmers coax their trees to bloom for New Year's Eve. The amount of blossom which opens in the house during the celebrations determines the wealth the household will acquire during the coming year, so accurate timing is essential.

Yuen Siu, the Spring Lantern Festival, falls on the fifteenth day of the New Year marking the end of the festivities. Also known as Chinese Valentine's Day, in the past it was the day when young unmarried girls would put on their best clothes and go out with their chaperones to meet eligible young men.

In Hong Kong more lanterns are seen at the Mid-Autumn Festival, also known as the Moon Festival, held on the fifteenth day of the eighth month of the lunar calendar. One of the many stories of the origin of this festival goes back to the fourteenth century revolt against the Mongols who held a certain walled city. One of the Chinese soldiers entered the city disguised as a Daoist priest and handed out cakes containing messages about the revolt. The soldiers then gathered that night with their torches and went to war. Taking the Mongols by surprise they won the battle and formed the basis of the Ming dynasty. On the evening of the festival, family picnics are held in parks or open spaces, eating moon cakes and surrounded by lighted lanterns. A children's parade takes place with lanterns representing the soldiers' torches now made in the form of rabbits, fish, birds and airplanes.

博古齋裝池

The Bun Festival held in May on the island of Cheung Chau is one of Hong Kong's favourite festivals. It dates from the plague epidemic of 1894 when islanders performed Daoist rites to drive off the disease and to placate the restless ghosts of those who died. Paper figures of deities are erected and a parade is held in which young children are dressed to represent characters from Chinese folklore. The ingeniously concealed framework makes the child appear to be floating at head height through the streets. The most spectacular symbols are three 16-metre towers made of bamboo and paper which are covered with sweet pink and white buns. Previously the young men of the island scrambled up the towers, but some years ago one of the towers collapsed and now the buns are handed out after the festivities.

香油

MOTORS

答
謝
神

The dragon boat festival is held on the fifth day of the fifth month of the lunar calendar. This major festival commemorates the death of a poet and national hero in China, Qu Yuen, who drowned himself in protest against a corrupt government during the 3rd century B.C. Villagers rowed towards him in a vain attempt to save him, beating their paddles to scare away the fish. Dumplings made of rice and meat were thrown into the water to feed the fish which would otherwise eat the body.

Today the festival is marked by narrow boats, with the head and the tail of a dragon, racing against each other with much symbolic beating of drums. Races are held in most of the fishing ports around the territory with everyone enjoying the holiday. The festival also attracts international teams from around the region.

HONG
KONG
JAPAN
1987

U R B A N   M O S A I C

City of contrasts, where else but in Hong Kong do classical colonial buildings crouch next to shiny skyscrapers? Where temples to Mammon tower over tiny roadside temples dedicated to a different god? Where the world's most expensive real estate houses designer boutiques and jewellery stores, while round the corner centuries' old trades remain? The *laissez faire* attitude of the colonial government allowed traditional customs to continue. A stable bureaucracy, coupled with the capacity for hard work and seizing opportunities by the incoming population, gave Hong Kong the perfect climate for entrepreneurs to prosper. The territory abounds with stories of penniless immigrants who made good and went on to become millionaires.

In the densely packed streets of the Central business district (facing page and below) smart secretaries, hotshot traders and tai tais *rub shoulders in the lunchtime crowds, each hurrying to the next opportunity. The rising population means the government must find more space, not easy on a tiny island. This results in constant reclamation of the harbour and low-rise buildings being replaced by skyscrapers.*

JCB
JCB CARD

80
Kodak is color
NORTH POINT
Kodacolor Film
Gold

The wealth and booming economy in recent years has made developers vie with each other to produce some of the most innovative architecture in Asia. Ultra-modern office buildings are designed by world famous architects such as I. M. Pei's towering triangular edifice for the new Bank of China (facing page, bottom left). But despite this, some traditions endure. Trams were introduced in 1904, and are still a favourite mode of transport today. They cover the 19-km stretch on the north face of Hong Kong island from Western district to Shaukiwan.

Above left: Across the harbour a plane glides over Kowloon City as it prepares to land at Kai Tak airport. Visitors to Hong Kong exceeded 10 million in 1995. Many of them arrived to do business in the territory.

Hong Kong is one of the major world financial markets. At the Stock Exchange in Exchange Square (bottom left) millions of dollars change hands daily. Traditional institutions like the HongKong Bank, Jardine's and Swire's plus more recently formed Chinese corporations all contribute greatly to the economy.

Hong Kong is a Shoppers Paradise and shopping here has been elevated to a high art. All the major international designers are represented in Central district and across the harbour in Tsimshatsui, doing a roaring trade with locals and visitors alike.

Seen from Chater Gardens the old Supreme Court Building is dwarfed by Princes Building, the Mandarin Oriental Hotel and Jardine House. The building, which dates back to 1903, now houses the Legislative Council at the political heart of Hong Kong.

A tram makes its stately way past the old Supreme Court while nearby, in the aviary in Hong Kong Park, birds fly oblivious to the crowds just over the trees.

Everyone likes to keep in touch. There are now nearly 900,000 mobile phones in use, and the number rises daily.

Two Hong Kong policemen survey the scene. Those wearing a red tag under the number on their shoulder epaulette can speak enough English to assist non-Chinese speakers.

Traditional Chinese architecture sits side by side with the most avant garde western buildings in Hong Kong (this page and facing page). The pastel coloured apartment block in Repulse Bay was designed with a hole in the centre to allow the lucky dragon to pass through. The hotel originally on the site was a sister hotel to the Peninsula on Kowloon. The famous Verandah Restaurant remains, seen nestling at the base of the apartment block. Shops and restaurants around the courtyard and garden are popular with both visitors and local people.

BREAK THE ICE
HARLEY-DAVIDSON
FK 19

The village of Stanley, on the south side of the island (facing page), attracts a younger crowd with its quirky mix of bars, restaurants, and street markets open every day selling souvenirs and inexpensive clothing. Over on Kowloon (above) the plaza outside the Cultural Centre is a convenient place to meet friends or just watch the world go by.

THE PENINSULA

THE PENINSULA
DT 5877

Standing at the tip of Kowloon the Peninsula Hotel was built in 1928, conveniently located for passengers taking the train from Kowloon station through China and beyond to Paris and London. Always at the centre of the social scene, it was a favourite rendezvous for visitors and locals alike. It is still the place to take tea in the graceful lobby, under the whirling ceiling fans, away from the heat and humidity. The hotel's fleet of dark green Rolls Royces conveys guests to the airport. Hong Kong holds the distinction of having the largest number of Rolls Royce per capita in the world.

Following pages: The glittering night-time view of Central district with the old Supreme Court building in the foreground, all lit up.

MALAYAN BANKING BHD.

Having worked hard and made money, the next thing to do is to spend it. There is never any problem in Hong Kong where it seems there is a shopping mall or fancy eating places on almost every street corner. Neon lights proclaim the latest and the greatest.
Facing page: One of the most unusual places to go is to the S.S. Whampoa, a concrete "ocean liner" anchored in a residential area of Whampoa Gardens in Hung Hom, once the site of the Admiralty Dockyards. Opened in 1989 it houses sports and recreation facilities as well as shops and restaurants. On Hong Kong island, Pacific Place (bottom left), is a more conventional, though no less popular haunt for the latest looks or gourmet treats.

WHAMPOA

The Hong Kong bride still favours the traditional Chinese wedding dress though her husband and the best man obviously prefer the latest western look (above left). Top right: A passenger is being "recorded" as the tram trundles along.

A rickshaw puller makes a meagre living posing for photographs while a young woman reads, totally oblivious of her surroundings.

Sometimes the old ways are still the best (facing page). Even the tallest high-rise blocks are erected using bamboo scaffolding and the skilful scaffolders are among the highest paid labourers. Bamboo also makes a useful pole on which to hang out the washing. Above left: The corner of Wellington Street and Lyndhurst Terrace was once the red-light district of Hong Kong in the 19th century. Above right: With most of Hong Kong island built against a mountain, life can sometimes be an uphill climb.

Street markets can be found all over the territory catering for every taste. The busy stalls in Wanchai (above right) and Central district (facing page) sell fresh produce and daily necessities while Stanley market (facing page, bottom left) and the night market in Temple Street (above left) are popular tourist spots with their inexpensive clothing and today's latest gimmick.

大字名店
Calvin Klein • ANDY & KAREN
69
金星
錄影帶
KENT

怡苑茶餐廳
咖啡紅茶 冷熱飲品 早午晚餐 精美飯盒 馳名咖喱 巧手小食 用料新鮮 歡迎外賣
電話:5453884 傳真:5454064

鋪位招租
APPLES
BLUE RIVER

The old trades still flourish, and the time-honoured method of weighing by catty persists despite government efforts to introduce the metric system. Street stalls offer a mix of food and daily necessities.

Chinese herbal stores dispense Chinese medicine which is preferred to western medicine. A herbalist will prescribe a potion to be made from a selection of herbs. The herbs are weighed carefully, chopped finely, then boiled in water. The broth is drained and drunk.

Fortune-tellers are consulted on all manner of decisions, when to get married, whether to buy more shares, or even which horse to back next Saturday. Small birds help the soothsayer by choosing the "right" paper.

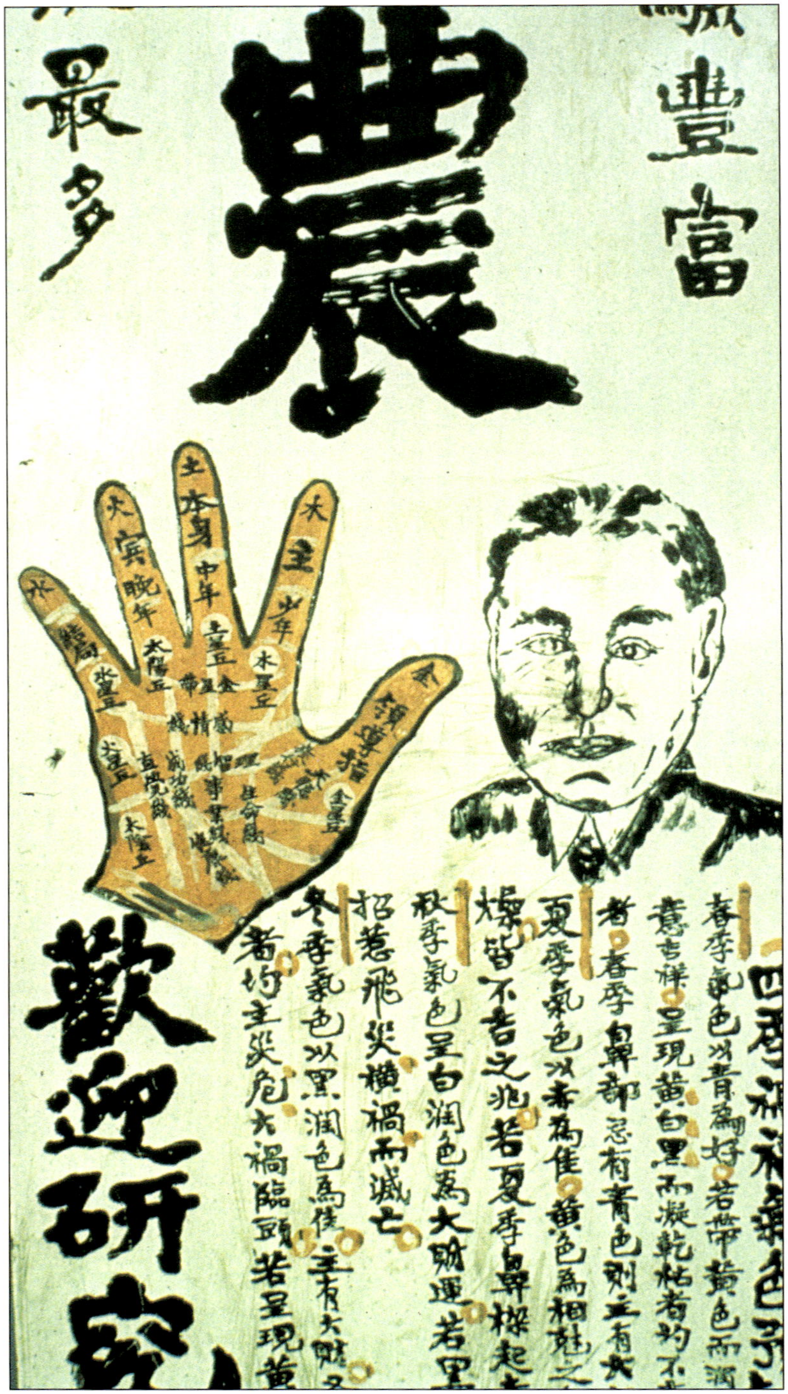

A portrait painter prepares a picture using a photo for guidance, while an old man polishes a brass container.

$28
$35

A shoemaker bends over his last while his wares are displayed above his head (left). Bird Street in Kowloon (facing page) is devoted to the sale of song birds and their cages. These cages are often expensive and intricately constructed. Hundreds of birds are on sale, the prices dependent more on their singing ability than their colourful plumage.

生貿易
TAK SANG
6 HONG LOK

LEISURE PLEASURES

Most Hong Kong people like to spend their leisure together. Not for them the deserted beach, or the quiet stroll through rolling hills. Instead, on weekends and public holidays in the cooler months, shopping malls and restaurants are bursting at the seams. When the temperature rises, so do the crowds on the beaches enjoying a barbecue or a swim. But for those who do want to get away from it all, majestic mountains or undulating parkland can easily be reached, and one can walk all day scarcely meeting another soul.

Many elderly Chinese men take their caged birds for a walk (facing page). Below: Teahouses have convenient hooks around the windows for owners to hang up the cages while having breakfast.

Chinese opera attracts a large audience. Magnificent costumes and highly stylised gestures recreate a world of emperors, fearless warriors and foolish villains. Make-up is an important part of the character's role. The noise is deafening as cymbals clash, drums roll and shrill falsettos bring back tales of Chinese mythology.

With more than 3,000 places to eat in Hong Kong, it is no wonder dining out is a favourite occupation. The choice ranges from inexpensive American fast food, British pubs and hawkers selling Chinese delicacies, through regional specialities, to the most expensive international restaurants.

Food stalls like the many dai pai dongs *are a cheap and convenient place for a quick and tasty meal. Apartments in Hong Kong can be very small and cramped, so many office workers and labourers will take all their meals in restaurants to save cooking at home. Neighbourhood cafes enjoy a good reputation with the local residents.*

Food from many regions of China is available in Hong Kong. But with most Hong Kong people hailing from Guangdong province where Guangzhou (Canton) is the major city, Cantonese cooking is the favourite. Food lovers can savour the delights of Cantonese dim sum, *those tasty snacks served in small bamboo baskets, rich and hearty Chiu Chow food, or seasonal delicacies such as freshwater hairy crabs from Shanghai trussed up with green straw, all washed down with a pot of Chinese tea.*

JUMBO
珍寶
珍寶海鮮舫
JUMBO FLOATING RESTAURANT

The Jumbo floating restaurant anchored in Aberdeen harbour (facing page) is open from sunrise to late into the night for classic Cantonese cooking and delicious dim sum. *Fresh seafood can be selected first from floating tanks.*
This page: British-style pubs often provide live entertainment in the evenings, while a hearty menu offers traditional "pub grub" and a pint all day long.

The shopping mall at the Landmark in Central has a host of upmarket boutiques and some convenient cafes to rest in after a serious shopping splurge.

Street musicians entertain the crowds while Filipinos on their Sunday off watch the entertainment in Statue Square. On that day the surrounding streets are closed to all traffic.

Racing is by far and away the most popular leisure activity for many Chinese. Punters intently watch the races at Happy Valley on Hong Kong island held on Wednesday evenings, and at Shatin in the New Territories on Saturday afternoons. Huge bets are placed, especially at the last race of the season at the end of June and well over HK$1 billion will be wagered that day.

Ocean Park near Aberdeen on the south side of the island is reached by one of the world's longest escalators or by the cable cars which swing out over the South China Sea. The combination of thrilling rides, the aquatic show featuring trained dolphins and a friendly killer whale, together with the panoramic views of distant Chinese islands make for a memorable day out (this page, facing and following pages).

228
79

Still, sometimes it's good just to get away from it all. Pull up the anchor and sail away, or simply lie on a sunny beach, and let the world go by. Tomorrow is another day.

COLIN

HONG KONG
1997

HONGKONG

THROUGH POSTCARDS

Hong Kong island in the late 19th century, the residential area already spreading up the sides of Victoria Peak.

Aberdeen on the south side of the island is one of the oldest fishing villages in Hong Kong (top). The busy harbour is home to a forest of tall-masted fishing junks as they rest between long sea voyages.
Bottom: Yaumati anchorage on the Kowloon Peninsula was a safe haven for boats during the frequent typhoons and summer monsoons.

The Star Ferry to Kowloon with Queen's Building on the far right and the Hong Kong Club in the background (top). The oldest club in the colony was first established in 1846 on the corner of Queen's Road and Wyndham Street. A refuge for taipans *and colonial officials, it excluded "shopkeepers, Chinese, Indians, women and other undesirables". This building was erected in 1897 and demolished in 1981 when it was replaced by a modern multi-storey building with the Club occupying the lower floors. Bottom: Queen's Building with the Hong Kong Club in the background on the left. The construction of Queen's Building, now the site of the Mandarin Oriental Hotel, was financed by an Armenian entrepreneur, Sir C.P. Chater, and the road alongside still bears his name. The harbour has been reclaimed many times since this picture was taken in the early years of this century and the buildings now stand well back from the shoreline.*

Most of the British population have turned out in style to hear Sir Henry Blake, Governor of Hong Kong from 1898-1903, proclaim Edward VII to be King of Great Britain and the Colonies, at a ceremony held in Royal Square in 1901 (top). Bottom: Hong Kong's first City Hall in its old location on Queen's Road was built by public subscription and opened in 1869. It contained a museum, a theatre and a public library. Demolished in stages, first in 1933 and the remainder in 1947, the present-day City Hall now stands on the waterfront near the Star Ferry and is still part of the cultural scene for the local community.

No. 15. Hongkong. Proclamation Day—Governor Blake proclaiming King Edward VII as King of Gt. Britain and Colonies

City Hall, Hongkong.

After Victoria Peak (top) opened for settlement in 1874, it became a retreat from the heat and the noise of the city below. Restricted at first to Europeans only, this was later modified by the Peak Reservation Ordinance of 1904 to those who met the approval of the Governor until 1930. Sir Robert Hotung, Jardine's comprador, was the first Chinese to live on the Peak. He had a large mansion for himself and one each for his two wives and children whom he would visit from time to time. Bottom : The Peak funicular railway opened in 1888 cutting the journey time from Central district from three hours, by sedan chair up difficult mountain paths, to just nine minutes. The first seat on the tram had a brass plaque, removed in 1949, stating it was reserved for the Governor, who retreated to his summer house on the Peak to enjoy the cooler temperatures.

The Peak tram is still regular commuter transport as well as a popular tourist attraction. Two trams are engaged to cover the steep journey, rising 395 metres above sea level. One tram descends as the other ascends and the two pass each other midway at the steepest gradient of one in two.

Bastion of commerce, the Hong Kong and Shanghai Bank has occupied the same location, One Queen's Road Central since 1865 (top). This gracious colonial building with classical Corinthian columns and a domed ceiling was completed in 1886. It was replaced in the 1980s with a futuristic design by architect Norman Foster epitomising the world's most expensive corporate headquarters.
Bottom: Jardine, Matheson & Co sugar factories at East Point, c.1880. After moving to Hong Kong from Guangzhou, Jardines centred their operations at East Point in 1841 and the first local sugar refinery was opened in 1878. A magnificent house and garden for the taipan *of Jardines was built on top of East Point Hill.*

Sikh police guard criminals in the stocks. Hong Kong's constabulary police, founded in 1844, comprised ex-British and Indian soldiers. The force was later expanded to include Chinese recruits.

Central Market (below) in Queen's Road was originally built in 1895 and rebuilt in its present style, as seen here, in 1938. The three-storey building extends through to Des Voeux Road and still functions today as a meat and vegetable market catering for many of the hundreds of restaurants in Hong Kong, as well as housewives in search of very fresh produce.

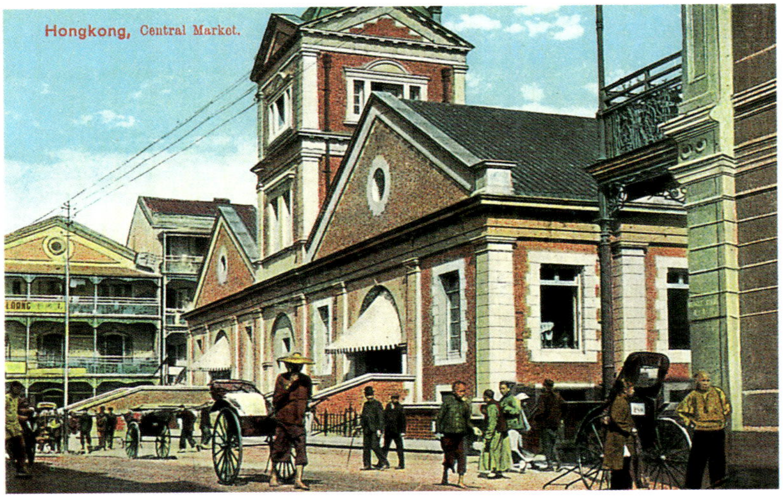

The heart of the city of Victoria, Pedder Street (right), with the prominent clock tower at the intersection with Queen's Road. The clock tower was donated by Douglas Lapraik who began his Hong Kong career as a watchmaker's assistant, and in true Hong Kong fashion, thirteen years later owned his own shipping company. The clock tower was completed in 1862 but demolished in 1913 as a traffic hazard.

Two views of Queen's Road. The top shows the Central section with the steps of Central Market just visible on the right. Below, in Queen's Road East, near the corner of Arsenal Street, the road is quieter as rickshaws make way for the old single decker tram trundling past.

When the racecourse opened at Happy Valley, both the Chinese and the British were avid gamblers and the annual races drew large crowds (top right). But tragedy struck on February 26, 1918 when strong winds fanned the flames which had broken out in the temporary mat-shed stands and 600 people perished in the inferno (below).

Sampan Street off Spring Gardens, itself a turning off Queen's Road East, was in one of the first residential areas on the island to be developed (right). Possibly named after the stream which still runs through it, the road survives as Spring Gardens Lane. Though originally built on the shoreline, reclamation now means it is sited well inland in present-day Wanchai.

A street in the infamous Kowloon Walled City. One of the conditions of the lease of the New Territories signed in 1898 was that Chinese magistrates stationed within the walled city of Kowloon should continue to exercise jurisdiction. The city later became a cramped, insanitary haven for criminals, prostitutes and drug addicts and a no-go area for Hong Kong police. In 1993 the land was handed back by China to the Hong Kong government and the rat-infested buildings torn down.

The Tin Hau Temple in Causeway Bay as seen in the late 1880s (top). There are more than forty temples in Hong Kong dedicated to the Daoist deity Tin Hau, the Queen of Heaven and Patron Saint of fisherpeople. The temple was originally built on the edge of the sea in Causeway Bay, but reclamation has placed Victoria Park in front and it is now well inland. Bottom: Opium smoking in the 19th century. First eaten raw as a medicine, the Chinese had smoked opium mixed with tobacco for hundreds of years. So it was seen as a natural choice in place of silver for western traders who brought it from India in exchange for Chinese tea, porcelain and silk.

Opium had been banned by the Chinese government in 1729 but without much attempt at enforcement as even the emperor's eunuchs and bodyguards were addicted. However the demand for the drug grew so high that it was a drain both physically and financially on the country and in 1839 Commissioner Lin was ordered by the Chinese government to seize 20,000 chests of opium and destroy them. The opium war which followed lasted until 1842, with the victorious British government claiming Hong Kong island as her own.

Street side stalls still proliferate today. Here in the 1930s, a hawker is proclaiming the freshness of his lychees, a juicy fruit popular in early summer, while another patiently perches by his cigarette stall.

A Chinese woman with bound feet (right). Footbinding was a barbaric custom which lasted for over 1,000 years and only died out in the early years of the 20th century. Women were not considered marriageable unless they had small feet of 12cm or less, and daughters had their feet bound from a very young age. The pain was described as never ending. Even some servants had bound feet and had to carry out many of their duties on their knees.*

Hongkong. Chinese High Class Ladies with small feet

A group of Chinese girls with small feet, taken at the end of the 19th century (above). Men found bound feet, called "golden lilies", titillating and the smell, when the bandages were removed, powerfully erotic.

HONGKONG. CHINESE WOMAN WITH BOUNDED FEET

Chinese boys "backing the book" (top). This was a standard method of learning in the 19th century where books based on the Chinese Classics must be committed to memory then recited out loud to the teacher. Bottom: Queen's Road West, the Chinese section of Hong Kong island, in about 1900. Rickshaws line the kerbside, while a coolie carries his load down the middle of the road.

The Gate in the old Kowloon Walled City leading to the magistrate's Yamen, his home and offices where he dispensed justice. It is now a 31,000 sq metre park modelled on a traditional Suzhou style garden. As a centrepiece, the magistrate's Yamen has been restored to its splendour of a century ago.